WITHDRAWN

Earthquakes

Catherine Chambers

www.heinemann.co.uk
Visit our website to find out more information about Heinemann Library books.

To order:
 Phone 44 (0) 1865 888066
 Send a fax to 44 (0) 1865 314091
Visit the Heinemann Bookshop at www.heinemann.co.uk to browse our catalogue and order online.

First published in Great Britain by Heinemann Library, Halley Court, Jordan Hill, Oxford OX2 8EJ
a division of Reed Educational and Professional Publishing Ltd. Heinemann is a registered trademark of Reed Educational & Professional Publishing Ltd.

OXFORD MELBOURNE AUCKLAND JOHANNESBURG BLANTYRE
GABORONE IBADAN PORTSMOUTH (NH) USA CHICAGO

Designed by Celia Floyd
Originated by Dot Gradations
Printed by Wing King Tong, in Hong Kong

04 03 02 01 00
10 9 8 7 6 5 4 3 2 1

ISBN 0 431 09605 8

British Library Cataloguing in Publication Data

Chambers, Catherine
Earthquake. – (Disasters in Nature)
1. Earthquakes – Juvenile literature
I. Title
551.2'2

Acknowledgements

The Publishers would like to thank the following for permission to reproduce photographs:

Camera Press: Itar - Tass Photo Agency pg.17; *Corbis*: pg.32, Tony Arruza pg.38, Vince Streano pg.22; *FLPA*: DP Wilson pg.40, Mark Newman pg.15, S McCutcheon pg.18, pg.25; *Magnum Photos*: George Rodger pg.43, Susan Meiselas pg.5; *Mary Evans*: pg.19; *Photri*: pg.39, pg.41; *Popperfoto*: pg.9; *Rex Features*: pg.7, pg.11, pg.34, pg.37, pg.44, pg.45; *Science Photo Library*: NASA pg.29; *Tony Stone*: Bob Thomas pg.27, Deborah Davis pg.16, Thomas Brase pg.31.

Cover photograph reproduced with permission of Robert Harding Picture Library.

Our thanks to Mandy Barker for her comments in the preparation of this book.

Every effort has been made to contact copyright holders of any material reproduced in this book. Any omissions will be rectified in subsequent printings if notice is given to the Publisher.

Any words appearing in the text in bold, **like this**, are explained in the Glossary.

Contents

Introduction

Under the Earth

Measuring and predicting

Living in the danger zone

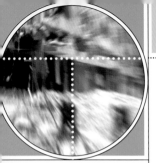

What is an earthquake?

The Earth's surface is constantly shifting. When the ground beneath us moves, it usually does it so slowly that we do not notice. Sometimes, however, it moves with such a huge force, sliding, slipping, shaking, sinking, that it cracks the Earth's surface. This is called an earthquake. There are thousands of earthquakes on the Earth's surface each year and there are many others deep in the Earth's crust that we do not feel. Some of these are measured by sensitive instruments called **seismometers**, placed deep in the ground, so we know that they occur. Out of about 3000 that we sense on the surface, only about ten will cause disasters.

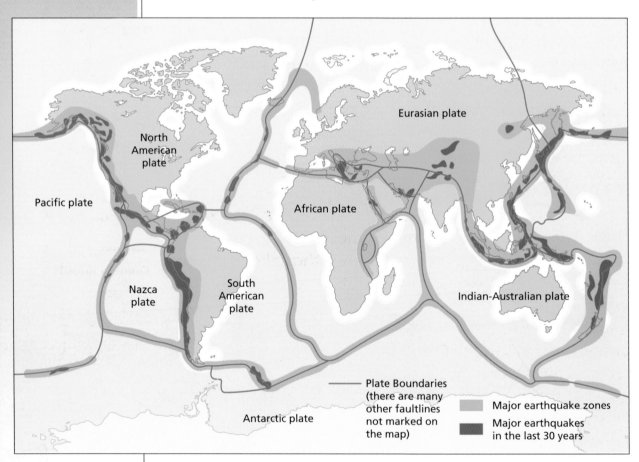

Eurasian plate

North American plate

Pacific plate

African plate

Nazca plate

South American plate

Indian-Australian plate

Antarctic plate

——— Plate Boundaries (there are many other faultlines not marked on the map)

Major earthquake zones

Major earthquakes in the last 30 years

This map shows how earthquake activity is related to the faultlines that separate the Earth's tectonic plates. However, an earthquake that begins on a faultline can cause tremors which affect the surface hundreds of kilometres away.

Where do earthquakes happen?

The Earth's crust is made of enormous **tectonic plates** which are pushing together or pulling apart all the time. Under the oceans, molten, sticky rock oozes from under the Earth's crust, creating ridges and mountains along the edges of the plates. As the edges of the plates grate together or slip and slide they cause the Earth to tremble. The worst affected areas of the world are China, Japan and other western Pacific islands, the west coast of the Americas, central Asia and the Mediterranean.

Earthquakes in our hands

It is far too late to stop people from living in areas affected by earthquakes, but we can try to construct our buildings, bridges, roads and railways so that they withstand most of the shock. We can also try to reduce the problems after the earthquake – the fires that rage and the services that grind to a halt.

Earthquakes on our minds

We hear about earthquake disasters regularly through the media, but we hear more quickly about disasters in some areas than others. Some earthquakes happen in very remote areas, or poor parts of the world where road networks and other **communications** are weak. This means that governments and international aid agencies are slow to react. Relief efforts are hindered because getting to the communities affected is difficult.

Mexico City's millions of citizens were totally unprepared for the earthquake disaster that struck on 19 September 1985. The disaster claimed about 10 000 lives.

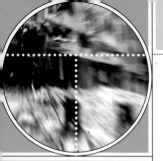

San Francisco – an earthquake disaster

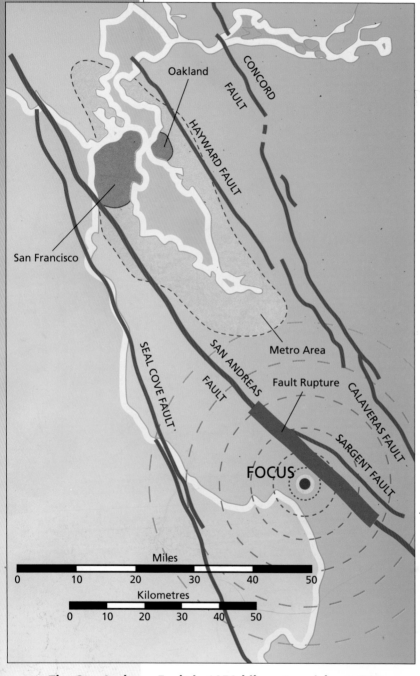

Oakland

CONCORD FAULT

HAYWARD FAULT

San Francisco

SEAL COVE FAULT

SAN ANDREAS FAULT

Metro Area

Fault Rupture

CALAVERAS FAULT

SARGENT FAULT

FOCUS

Miles
0   10   20   30   40   50

Kilometres
0   10   20   30   40   50

The San Andreas Fault is 1050 kilometres (about 660 miles) long. The 1989 earthquake re-opened a section of a 430-kilometre (269-mile) rift made during the devastating tremor that rocked San Francisco in 1906.

About 96 kilometres (60 miles) south of San Francisco, at 5.04 p.m. on 17 October 1989, a section of the San Andreas fault system slipped. Part of the Loma Prieta Peak in the Santa Cruz mountains suddenly lurched 2 metres (6 feet) northward. A huge crack 40 kilometres (25 miles) long split open the earth in two directions. Just 6 seconds later the shock waves hit San Francisco Bay to the north. For 15 long seconds the ground shook. Buildings tumbled, electricity cables and gas pipes were severed and fires broke out. Roads and bridges collapsed. Sixty-eight people were killed and 3757 were injured. The emergency services were stretched to their limits.

How did it happen?

The San Andreas faultline separates the North American and Pacific **tectonic plates** and runs all the way from north-west California to the Gulf of California. For several days before the earthquake, a lot of small tremors had been registered in the area and scientists believed that a 'big one' was due. The plates normally slide past each other quite smoothly, causing only faint tremors, but there are some parts that jam against each other as they slide, building up stresses that are eventually released as an earthquake. This is exactly what happened on 17 October. The 15 second quake reached 7.1 on the **Richter scale** which is high (see page 23).

Where did the damage occur?

Most of the damage occurred in the Marina District near the coast. The buildings worst affected were those built on soft ground, such as floodplains – flat areas of fine silt around rivers as they widen towards the sea. Landfill sites were also badly hit. These areas were once lagoons – coastal inlets of water protected by raised sandbanks. The lagoons had been filled in with rubble and then built upon. As the tremors vibrated, the soft, loose ground began to move around like a liquid, making the buildings on top of it sink or shake even more. This is known as the **liquefaction** effect.

The San Francisco earthquake of 1989 destroyed 1018 homes and damaged 23 408.

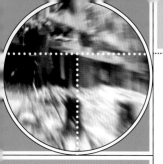

After the disaster

Who paid for the damage?

It took a long time for San Francisco's politicians to fund the repairs to **infrastructures** such as roads and bridges. Immediate repairs often have to be paid for with money borrowed from banks and other financial institutions, which charge interest on the loans. This means that the borrower has to pay back a lot more money than the repair job actually cost.

Many homes and businesses claimed repair money through their **insurance policies** but some people had not taken out insurance or not one that covered damage done by earthquakes. The problem of who pays out for repairs is a huge one in the United States, which suffers a great range of natural disasters from annual hurricanes and tornadoes, floods, drought and even the occasional volcano. In some parts of the country it simply costs too much to be insured against natural disasters at all.

Waiting for the next one

When the San Andreas fault was inspected it was found that the crack had opened up on the southern-most part of a rip that had occurred in 1906. This, too, had toppled San Francisco, destroying half of the city. It had taken 83 years for pressure to build up from this 'locked' section of the San Andreas fault and be released as an earthquake. This same fracture – although not exactly the same **epicentre** – with its carbon copy 'hit' on San Francisco was the starting point for scientists trying to work out when the next 'big one' would occur. The task now is to examine the forces put upon the mountains by the same clash of **tectonic plates** and to try to estimate how long it will take for pressure to build up again.

Pressure points

- In the year following the disaster, 7000 more shocks were recorded in the San Francisco area.
- Five of the shocks measured more than 5.0 on the **Richter scale** and 40 measured more than 4.0.

Aid and arguments

It often takes a disaster like this to show the real needs of a city and to get people to take action. The emergency services responded quickly and efficiently to the San Francisco earthquake. Nevertheless, their work was hampered by a lack of resources. In February 1990, the San Francisco Firefighters' Union mounted a protest at budget cuts that had stopped them from effectively tackling the fires following the earthquake, and from rescuing people trapped by fallen buildings. The firefighters presented 70 000 signatures to the Registrar of Voters to show how many people supported their plea for more resources. The President of the Union said, 'The havoc it (the earthquake) wrought showed just how thin our forces have been spread since the budget cuts.'

After the San Francisco 1906 earthquake, a lot of thought went into rebuilding the city. Research and development into specialized earthquake-resistant architecture had taken place not only in the United States but also in other earthquake zones, especially Japan.

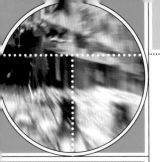

Hitting the headlines

Which earthquakes make the headlines? Why do some parts of the world get more media attention than others? And why is too much coverage not always appreciated?

Positive and negative

Pictures of the San Francisco earthquake were soon televised by satellite around the world. These images attracted the attention of millions of people and prompted many offers of assistance, which continued well into the following year. In February 1990, San Francisco's sister city, Taipei, on an island near China, donated £62 500 (US$100 000) to the earthquake disaster fund. Taipei City itself lies in an earthquake zone, so its people were sympathetic.

A month earlier, and only three months after the disaster, business leaders had been complaining that worldwide coverage of the earthquake had projected an image of total devastation. Pictures of rubble and burning buildings which made it look as if the whole city had gone up in smoke. The tourist industry had been especially badly affected. This led the spokeswoman for the Convention and Visitors' Bureau to plea for the promotion of a more positive image of the city. She pointed out that the area worst affected was the Marina district – not the Wharf, where visitors could still receive the highest standards of hospitality.

Choosing stories

It is sometimes quite puzzling why one earthquake hits the headlines, but another similar one does not. Some earthquakes occur in very remote or poor places. Road and **communication** networks are often bad – journalists and aid agencies find it difficult to reach the disaster zone. Also, some governments may not want the outside world to be looking at them so they try to cope alone.

Worldwide, what happens in some countries is considered more important than what goes on in others. A superpower such as the United States of America is watched by the rest of the world all the time. Foreign media networks have journalists posted permanently in Washington, the US capital. North America's excellent road and air communication networks enable camera crews to reach other parts of the States almost as soon as a disaster occurs.

The earthquake which struck Tangshan city in China on 28 July 1976 was so violent that people were thrown 2 metres (6 feet) into the air. Altogether, over 230 000 people lost their lives. But at that time, China's government was not popular in many parts of the world, especially in the United States and western Europe, so this particular earthquake was never fully reported by the international media.

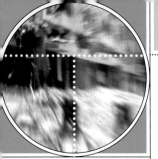

Waves beneath our feet

Earthquakes occur mostly along great splits that divide the Earth's crust into huge masses of land called **tectonic plates**. Splits, or faultlines, are where the plates shift at the rate of several centimetres each year – the different types of faulting are shown in the diagram below. The plates do not always glide smoothly past each other. Sometimes they suddenly catch and then break free creating **shock waves** that rise to the surface. Several thousand of these are felt as earthquakes above ground every year, while many thousands more go undetected.

The faultlines do not go all the way round the tectonic plates. They tend to form a jagged line, from smaller sections of rifts or tears, and these are not always connected. The San Francisco earthquake of 1989, for example, was caused by a sudden movement along just a section of the San Andreas Fault, not along its whole length. Sometimes, parts of the fault get stuck, and the pressure builds up for many years until the rock just cannot take it any more. Then the Earth quakes.

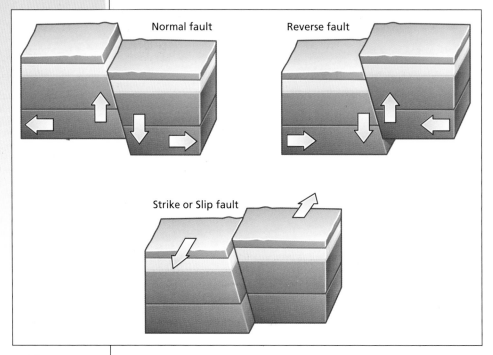

Normal fault

Reverse fault

Strike or Slip fault

Some faults slip down, some are thrust upwards, while others slide along each other without moving up or down at all.

How the fault shifts

The huge forces created by a moving fault change the shape of the rock on either side. When the strain is too great, the force is released in shock waves that cause a sudden movement along the fault. If the shock waves are strong the Earth's crust will break. This relieves the pressure on the crust, and the rock, although cracked, is no longer buckled or twisted.

The movement begins deep down at a point called the **focus**, and is released at a point directly above it called the **epicentre**. This is the point from which the waves of energy push outwards until the force they create cracks open the surface.

Where the Earth moves

The crust itself is cold and brittle, so it breaks quite easily. But under this crust, about 30 kilometres (20 miles) beneath the surface at its thinnest point, is a hot, sticky, supple layer, called the **mantle**, which is wrapped around the core of the Earth like a soft cushion. The tectonic plates move around slightly on top of it all the time. Some earthquakes occur where the plates collide, or press against each other continually. Most earthquakes, and the largest, occur in the Earth's **subduction zones**. These are where one plate dips below another, towards the layer of sticky **magma**, as we can see in the diagram.

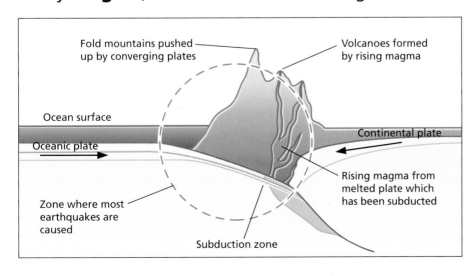

Fold mountains pushed up by converging plates

Volcanoes formed by rising magma

Ocean surface

Oceanic plate

Continental plate

Rising magma from melted plate which has been subducted

Zone where most earthquakes are caused

Subduction zone

Earthquakes occur where one plate slips down under the other. The crust melts as it falls down into the magma – the molten rock that forms the mantle.

What's in a wave?

The waves of energy that make the Earth tremble and crack are called **seismic waves**. 'Seismic' comes from a Greek word meaning 'to shake'. Each has its own **frequency**, which is a number that counts the waves passing the same point within a certain time. Each has its own strength. Seismic waves are not all the same, they make different patterns as they move. All these things give waves their own characteristics and tell us the kind of impact they will make. One of the most important things that affect the way seismic waves move is the material through which they pass.

All waves travel faster and keep to a regular pattern when they move through very hard material, such as **granite** rock. This is because hard rock has a rigid, uniform texture. Soft materials such as river **sediment**, and soil, have a more movable and varied texture. This means that waves travel more slowly, but they **interfere** with other waves more easily.

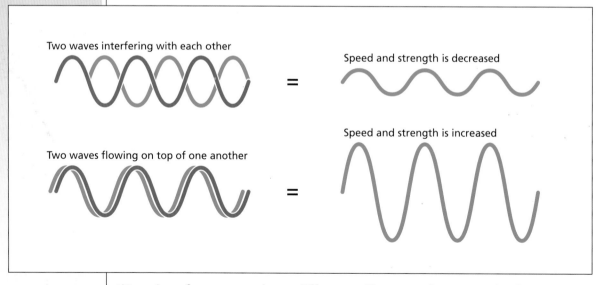

Two waves interfering with each other = Speed and strength is decreased

Two waves flowing on top of one another = Speed and strength is increased

Wave interference can have different effects on the strength of an earthquake. When two waves flow on top of each other their strength and speed is increased and the quake will be stronger. But when a peak of one wave meets the trough of another, the waves are interfering with each other. This makes them slower and weaker.

Making patterns

The two main groups of wave are **body waves** and **surface waves**. Body waves move through bodies of solid, consistent rock. There are two different types, known as **pressure waves**, and **shear waves**. Pressure waves move lengthways through the material, in the direction of the final quake. Shear waves move at right angles to it.

Surface waves move along the irregular parts of rock structures – the bands and layers made up of different rock types, or the places where they meet with more solid material. Because the different waves move at different speeds, **seismologists** can measure and compare their speed and direction, and work out an earthquake's **epicentre**.

Energy waves would have a difficult journey through this rock, which has many layers of different types, textures and densities.

Pressure points

- Seismic waves are most damaging when they come from a shallow **focus** less than 30 kilometres (18 miles) beneath the Earth's surface.

- The next most damaging occur from a medium depth of 50–80 kilometres (30–50 miles).

- The least damaging are those rippling from a deep focus, more than 80 kilometres (50 miles) beneath the Earth's surface.

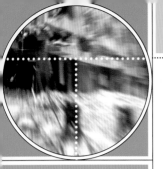

Moving the Earth

Sections of the Earth's crust move all the time. While scientists can measure the few centimetres that they shift each year, most of us cannot see where movement has occurred. This type of movement is known as **fault creep**. There are few signs of it on the landscape because the energy waves are too slow and weak, but sudden fault movement causes violent waves of energy that fracture and fold the landscape.

Changing the landscape

As we can see from the picture, earthquakes can cause dramatic sideways movement on the Earth's surface. Before the earthquake, the road and the land around it were at rest. The road ran in a straight line. In the second stage, pressure was put on the road so that it probably bulged slightly. In the third stage, sudden movement in the Earth's crust made the road rupture and slip. Now in its last stage, the split road is at rest again. This is known as **offset** and can affect bridges and railway lines in the same way. The same movement also divides rivers so that they have to make a new **channel**. The lower parts of the rivers can be left with no direct source of water. They may dry up leaving pools and lakes, and then just empty, waterless valleys.

This road is offset, and has experienced **elastic rebounding**. The road and the earth beneath it have rebounded into a different formation.

Earth tremors can also cause **subsidence**, when part of the ground suddenly sinks. It appears on the surface as a steep step in a rock, and it splits the level of roads, railways or bridges, making them impassable. If the ground beneath a river or stream subsides, the water will cascade steeply over the lip of the top half, making a waterfall or a rapid.

The diagram on page 12 shows an example of a **reverse fault**. This type of fault, which slopes backwards, is often hidden. When it moves it does not show cracks on the surface. Instead, it folds the ground above it into huge, wavy layers of rock. Some reverse fault earthquakes can cause ripples and ridges on the surface, or mounds of earth. The folds caused by reverse fault movement do have some advantages. On the edge of Coalinga, in California, a huge underground petroleum oil reservoir has been folded upwards over millions of years by the reverse faultline beneath it. The townspeople were unaware that this is how their pool of oil was formed, until an earthquake struck in May 1983.

As tremors split and crack the ground, they also break water pipes flooding buildings and weakening their structure still further. Sewage pipes fracture so waste water mixes with clean water. Roads and other **communications** are completely disrupted.

Tsunami!

The map on page 4 shows that many of the Earth's major faultlines run along the coastlines and across the ocean floor. This means that tremors often occur near water, or right underneath it. Far from stopping the tremor, oceans and seas allow the **seismic waves** to pass through them – but not without causing a bit of a stir.

Walls of water

A **tsunami** is a parade of waves, some rising only a few centimetres above normal levels and others as tall as a block of flats. They are often called tidal waves but this name is misleading, as they are nothing to do with tides at all. Tsunamis are caused mostly by earthquakes, although sometimes volcanic activity under the ocean can cause them too. As the water is moved by a tremor, the swell of water makes waves across the surface. These become faster and more powerful as they travel, until they crash ashore. Across the deep Pacific Ocean these waves can travel at about 700 kilometres per hour (435 miles per hour). When they reach the coast, the resistance of the upward slope slows them down – the waves build up high and topple over onto the shore.

The enormous power of a tsunami can carry massive objects ashore and devastate the coast.

Wide, open and deep shorelines usually suffer little from tsunamis. A wave will rise only very slightly, almost unseen. Buoys and small boats might rock gently, and sand and shingle might be pushed a little way up the beach but there will be no real danger from the wave.

On the other hand, curved, shallow bays concentrate the strength of the tsunami, making it squeeze into a smaller space. This boosts the height of the wave and the speed at which it hits the shore. They can rise 30 metres (about 98 feet) high and can hit land at 250 kilometres per hour (about 160 miles per hour). People who are in the way are completely **submerged** or dragged out to sea by the powerful undercurrent. Buildings are crushed, trees are snapped in half or uprooted, and boats are shattered into splinters.

In 1755, a great earthquake measuring about 8.5 on the **Richter scale** flattened Lisbon, the capital of Portugal. It was followed just 40 minutes later by a huge tsunami which was probably more than 15 metres (50 feet) high.

Pressure points

- Most tsunamis are caused by earthquakes with **foci** less than 50 kilometres (about 30 miles) below the ocean floor.

- Most tsunamis are caused by earthquakes above a **magnitude** of 6.5 on the Richter scale.

- Most deadly tsunamis have foci less than 25 kilometres (about 16 miles) below the surface of the ocean floor.

Rumbling and erupting

The Earth's crust rumbles and cracks as it slips and slides over the layer of sticky **magma** beneath. The Earth's movement also affects the magma itself, so it pushes up through weak points and **fissures** in the crust, making volcanoes. Some volcanoes form deep down on the ocean floor, while others break through the surface of the sea, solidifying into islands. Over millions of years, many have made chains of mountains on the edges of continents. As the map shows, a lot of these run along the edges of **tectonic plates**, in exactly the same places as earthquake activity. Volcanic eruption is not always explosive. Sometimes magma moves slowly upwards and oozes out like treacle. As it travels up the **conduit**, this red-hot magma cracks the inside surface of the rock, causing tremors.

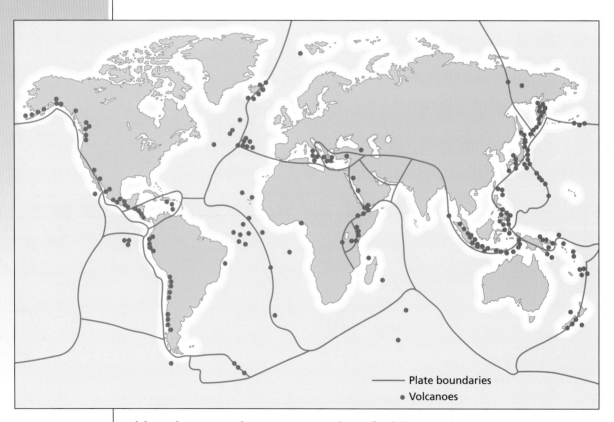

— Plate boundaries
• Volcanoes

Although many volcanoes erupt along faultlines, others seem to pop out of nowhere. These volcanoes push up through 'hotspots' – areas where the Earth's crust is thin.

Tell-tale tremors

The ground around a volcano often rumbles for hours or even days before an eruption. **Vulcanologists** take a great interest in any earth tremors that occur on or around a resting volcano. In March 1980, in the US state of Washington, Mount St Helen's awoke with a small eruption, after being dormant (inactive) for 137 years. This was followed by two months of earth tremors that produced a 5-kilometre (3-mile) crack in the side of the volcano. They watched, too, as magma slowly pushed out a bulge on the north-east slope. These studies enabled them to predict that Mount St Helen's would at some point soon produce 'the big one'. In May 1980, Mount St Helen's erupted so fiercely that a huge hole was blasted in its north-east face.

A vulcanologist called Milton Garces is developing a new way of predicting volcanic eruptions. From the surface of the crater he measures changes in **infrasound** – minute wavelengths of sound that humans cannot even hear. These vibrate right from the **magma chamber**, up through the conduit and into the **vent**.

Movements in the Earth's crust release magma, upwards through the volcano. It also finds its way through weak points – fissures, or cracks in the crust.

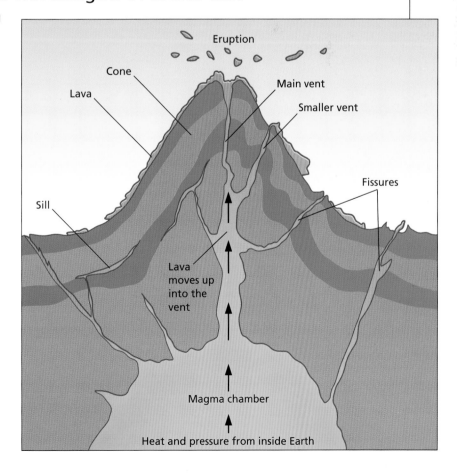

Eruption

Cone

Lava

Main vent

Smaller vent

Fissures

Sill

Lava moves up into the vent

Magma chamber

Heat and pressure from inside Earth

Measuring and predicting
Mighty measurements

How do we measure earthquakes? How do we know when 'the big one' will strike? We can only really answer the first of these questions properly. Measuring the strength of earthquakes, finding their **epicentre** and tracking their spread are all parts of the science of **seismology** – the study of earthquakes.

Pressure points

These are some of the instruments used to measure earthquakes.

- **Seismometer** – a very sensitive instrument that picks up the pattern of ground tremors and traces them on a paper roll or magnetic tape. The continual pattern makes a **seismograph**.

- Two of the different kinds of seismometer use a swinging pendulum or an electromagnetic galvanometer, an instrument which measures **electromagnetic** currents, to pick up the tremors – even very slight ones.

- **Accelerometers** are instruments that only work when the tremor is huge – they are not sensitive to small movements but they are much stronger than seismometers, which can be destroyed in a large earthquake.

A **seismologist** is reading a seismograph, which is recording tremors registered on a seismometer. One of the problems of seismometers is that they are very sensitive, but they have to be able to withstand violent tremors, too.

The Richter scale

The earthquake measurements given in this book are all on the **Richter scale** (below). It was invented by the American seismologist, Dr Charles Richter in 1935 and gives values for the amount of energy released by **seismic waves** that radiate from the epicentre (see page 13). This is the **magnitude**. Each **intensity** of magnitude – the number on the scale – is ten times more powerful than the one before it, and each intensity can be linked to the amount of destruction it causes.

Magnitude	Effect
1	Cannot be felt on the surface and can only be detected by instruments near the epicentre
2	Can be felt only slightly near the epicentre
3	Can be felt near the epicentre but causes little damage
4-5	Can be felt at a distance of about 30 kilometres (20 miles) from the epicentre and can cause some damage in small areas
6	Can be clearly felt over a wide area and can cause a fair amount of damage
7	Buildings fall, people are killed, damaging **tsunamis** can be generated
8	An earthquake disaster strikes, also tsunami disaster, widespread devastation

It is very difficult to describe exactly what will happen when an earthquake of a particular magnitude strikes, but some seismologists have studied the effects of different intensities of magnitude in much greater detail, as we shall see on the next page.

More measurements

Scientists had realized that, however much shaking and rumbling took place, it was the size of the surface fracture that mattered most. A small fracture would generally cause less damage than a large one. Of course, the impact on humans also depends on what they have built on top of the fracture.

Measuring the damage

Some scales include not only seismic measurements but also what people can actually feel and see during an earthquake. This can be very useful if it is compared with the other scales, and linked to the type of ground and structures built on it. It helps to predict what might happen in an earthquake of a particular size in a particular place, even if it isn't useful for earthquake prediction itself.

In 1966, the Japanese seismologist, Kei Aki created a measuring system based on **seismic motion**. This calculation included not just surface movement and damage but also the duration of the tremor – how long it lasts – and the amount of fault movement.

Probably the best scale of this type was developed by Giuseppi Mercalli in 1902. He established twelve different grades of damage to buildings, roads and other infrastructures. Over the next 30 years, these scales went out of date. More electric cables, telegraph lines and power stations had been built – the motorcar and bus had replaced the horse and carriage – and more roads and bridges had been made to carry them. Two other scientists, Wood and Neumann, helped to revise the scale, which is now known as the Mercalli-Wood-Neumann scale. It is one of the most trusted measurements of surface damage and is still widely used today.

Pressure points

This is Grade 8 on the Mercalli-Wood-Neumann scale, and shows some of the kinds of things that are considered.

Damage is slight in specially designed structures; considerable in ordinary, substantial buildings, with partial collapse; great in poorly-built structures. … Fall of chimneys, factory stacks, columns, monuments … Heavy furniture overturned. … Changes in water levels in wells. Earthquake disturbs persons who are driving motor cars.

A worldwide web

Computers are now used to analyse data collected by more traditional earthquake-measuring devices such as **seismometers**. Computer technology is also being linked to satellite communications to create a worldwide earthquake study system. This is focused on stations in three earthquake zones – Africa, Antarctica and South America. The system is called the **Global Telemetred Seismograph Network**.

One of the biggest earthquakes ever, measuring 8.4 on the **Richter scale** shattered the town of Anchorage in Alaska in 1964, causing massive landslides and a **tsunami** that reached as far as the Californian coast.

Seeking tsunamis

The tremors of a **magnitude** 8 earthquake in the middle of an ocean might not affect anyone living on land directly, but it could cause a huge **tsunami**. Tsunamis are silent until they strike. Without monitoring and warning systems, they take people completely by surprise. The most vulnerable communities live on small islands, especially those in the Pacific Ocean.

A centre for tsunami-spotting

In the United States, half a million people live in the path of tsunamis reaching 15 metres (about 50 feet) high, while over a million are at risk of suffering tsunamis towering over 30 metres (about 100 feet). Most of these occur in the US Hawaiian Islands, which have been battered by over 170 tsunamis in the last 200 years – that's almost one every year!

Pressure points

Japan has invested a lot of time and money in developing ways of preventing tsunami disaster ...

- building **breakwaters** and zig-zag concrete sea-walls – concrete barriers that break the waves as they hit the shore
- building sea-front hotels on concrete stilts so that water rushes between the pillars and underneath the hotel rooms
- moving homes, shops and offices inland away from danger
- building several roads leading inland away from the shore. This ensures that people can escape easily and quickly, without panic and accidents, when a tsunami warning is given.

Hawaii is a real hotspot. Not only do its own earthquakes and volcanoes make their own tsunamis, it also lies in the path of tsunamis generated far away across the sea. Because Hawaii lies at the heart of tsunami action, in 1946 the United States' National Oceanographic and Atmospheric Administration chose Hawaii to set up the **Pacific Tsunami Warning System** (PTWS). Seismic and tide stations monitor the Pacific Basin from all the major harbours in the region.

Hawaii's sophisticated tsunami warning system alerts people to even the smallest risk – but do they take any notice? Some people have been **evacuated** many times from a beach, to find out later that only tiny tsunamis trickled onto the sands. People stop worrying about warnings and are more reluctant to hurry away from a danger spot.

Tools of the trade

The main instruments used to detect and measure tsunami waves are the **seismograph**, which measures the kinds of movement that will spark off a tsunami wave, and the **tide gauge**, which measures the height of waves. A tide gauge is a float set in a vertical tank of water in a sheltered area like a harbour. The float rises and falls as the water swells and dips. A measuring instrument is attached to the float and records its movement. Their position makes them poor as prediction tools as they can only measure the wave as it is about to strike. Computers can now be used to collect all these statistics and build up a picture of how waves behave and the impact they make at landfall.

Imperfect predictions

All the statistics gathered on earthquakes throughout the world have not yet led to a major breakthrough in earthquake prediction. The problem is that the beginnings of earthquakes all seem to be the same, so we cannot tell what will happen at the end of the shock's journey by studying its beginning. We cannot warn people in time because the origins of earthquakes tell us nothing about the effects they will have when they reach the surface.

In recent years, scientists in California have been concentrating on isolating the characteristic of a beginning that will lead to a 'big one'. There are ten to twelve earth tremors in and around Los Angeles every day. Nothing so far has enabled **seismologists** to distinguish between their origins. They needed to monitor a tremor right from its beginning to its end. So they set up.

The Parkfield experiment

Parkfield is a town in California that experiences a large earthquake roughly every 22 years. The origin and track of the quakes is thought to be always more or less the same. An earthquake was expected to hit Parkfield just before 1993, so scientists from the United States Geological Survey visited the site and drilled holes deep down into the crust. Here, they placed **seismometers**, while on the surface they set up lasers that projected beams from one building to another. This was to measure any movement of the buildings and therefore any shift in the ground. These and other instruments worked constantly, watching for the earthquake. The scientists waited eagerly. At last they were in a position to track an earthquake from its beginning to its end. 1993 came and went – so did 1994 – and no earthquake. They're still waiting!

Making maps

Scientists try to develop **hazard maps** of areas likely to be hit. Some of these are based on the length of time it takes for shifting movements of fault sections finally to move the boundary between **tectonic plates** in a big earthquake. It's a bit like a conveyor belt shuffling along to the end of the production line. The length of time it takes for the small shifts to end in a big bang is known as the 'seismic gap'. Seismologists estimate how long it will take for this seismic cycle to repeat itself.

This prediction method is not very accurate – it cannot pinpoint exactly when an earthquake will occur. It also only applies to quakes along the edges of tectonic plates, and the method tends to divert attention from other areas at risk. In Japan in the 1970s, all eyes were on the Tokai area south of Tokyo, which was thought to be nearing the end of its seismic cycle – a big quake might soon occur. Instead, an earthquake shook the other side of Japan, killing 106 people.

This coloured satellite radar image shows the Hector Mine earthquake on 16 October 1999 in California. The coloured bands show displacement of ground, with the tightest bands at the **epicentre**. This earthquake measured 7.1 on the **Richter scale**.

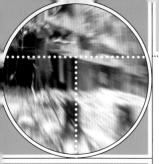

Senses versus science

A huge quake struck the Japanese city of Kobe in 1965, 400 years after the last big one, which was recorded by Buddhist monks. Six thousand people died in this earthquake and, ever since, predicting the next one has been top priority. But while Japan has the most expensive and up-to-date earthquake prediction systems in the world, they have yet to predict a major earthquake accurately!

Strange changes

In Kobe, prediction tools include satellite images, which are supposed to show movements in the Earth's crust. Ten days before the next major earthquake struck in 1995, these tools failed to show any changes, although during this time, strange changes were seen in the sky, which turned from red to green to blue. The people of Kobe noticed unusual things happening in their homes, too. The hands of electric clocks dropped down towards the 6. Air conditioners began to stop and start on their own. Television channels switched from one to another without so much as a button being pressed. At night, the moon blushed – it was pink!

After ten days the quake struck. No one had been **evacuated** because the scientific instruments had not indicated that an earthquake was imminent. Afterwards, scientists began to analyse the strange stories that had flooded in over the past few days. They decided that changes in the Earth's **electromagnetism** had caused some of these phenomena. They linked it to observations made some way away in the city of Kyoto, where scientists had noticed severe electric storms with blinding lightning. So what should we take notice of – science or senses?

Sensitive creatures

In China one ancient method which is still used to predict earthquakes is the study of animal behaviour. This method has been dismissed by scientists in some other parts of the world, but in February 1975, in Haicheng, **hibernating** snakes rose from their nests in the middle of winter. **Seismologists** used this information, together with other statistics, to predict an earthquake successfully. Haicheng was evacuated and hundreds of thousands of lives were saved.

Human instinct

Some people living in earthquake zones believe that symptoms such as sickness, dizziness, headaches and heart palpitations are all indications that the Earth is about to crack. It would be easy to dismiss these claims but, as we have seen, changes in electrical and magnetic forces as well as deep stirrings in the Earth's crust affect the delicate instruments that scientists have created. Our bodies, too, are delicate instruments. Can they also detect the changes?

A number of scientists use **hot springs** to help them predict earthquakes. Some **geysers**, such as Old Faithful in the United States, erupt very regularly. When their pattern changes, it is an early sign that the earth underneath is moving.

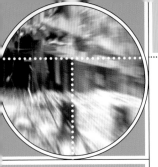

Getting out of the way

There is no way of preventing earthquakes. Predicting them is not an exact science as yet. Fleeing from them is virtually impossible. So is it possible to warn people?

A ray of hope

A new warning system developed along the San Andreas Fault in California is helping people to get out of the way. The warnings do not give enough time for people to escape from the area, but they do give a chance to get out of a building that could crumble or catch fire. When fast, strong tremors are picked up, an automatic warning light flashes in earthquake centres around the region.

Tremors can travel as fast as 7 kilometres (4.4 miles) per second – faster than the speed of sound. Slower tremors can travel at about 3.2 kilometres (2 miles) per second. This gives people living 160 kilometres (100 miles) away from the **epicentre** between 20 and 50 seconds to get out of the way, if they are warned. In 1994, in Mexico City, this was enough to **evacuate** many people from city centre buildings successfully.

The worst effects of earthquakes upon people are fire and falling buildings like here in the San Francisco earthquake of 1989. So it is vital that the fire service is able to function quickly and efficiently.

Weary of warnings?

Every year there are about 30 000 tremors in the US state of California alone. In June 1988, a **magnitude** 5 tremor hit an area about 80 kilometres (50 miles) from San Francisco. A public warning was issued because it was thought that an even bigger tremor would soon strike. What were people supposed to do? No one knew whether a big earthquake would strike within days or even months. Life, work – and even school – just have to go on! Early in 1989 another public warning was given. A few months later, San Francisco was struck by a magnitude 7.1 earthquake (see page 6). No one could have been prepared for the exact moment at which it struck. No one could have moved away from the city for a whole year, just waiting for it!

Pressure points

As we have seen, **tsunamis** follow after earth tremors, which makes them easier to predict and track. This also makes warnings and evacuations easier.

- It takes three hours to evacuate a city the size of Honolulu in the US island state of Hawaii, so tsunami warnings have to be made well in advance.

- It costs £18.75 million (US$30 million) to evacuate a city the size of Honolulu. This makes false alarms very expensive.

- In California, computer predictions have worked out that a large earth tremor on the Santa Catarina faultline will cause a dangerous tsunami eight minutes later. It will probably strike just north of Los Angeles airport.

- Scientists from the University of California want **hazard maps** to be published in all telephone directories. If a tsunami strikes, this will enable people to find a safe place well out of the way.

33

Why live in danger?

Thirty per cent of the world's largest and fastest-growing cities lie in the most dangerous earthquake zones. That means a total of 600 million people are living in the way of earthquakes. Why? The map on page 4 shows earthquake zones are huge. Many of these zones are strung along the coastlines of continents where fishing communities have grown, and port cities have developed crucial trade links with the rest of the world.

In the Mediterranean region, ancient cities show how civilizations grew up along important trade routes. These ran from the Far East to the west of Europe, and right across the Sahara into West Africa. Such cities developed because they were quite simply in the most fruitful places to live – the threat of earthquakes was a small consideration. Serious earthquakes actually do not happen in exactly the same place that often. Often a disaster doesn't strike for several generations.

The hilltop village of Calabritto in southern Italy, was struck by an earthquake on 23 November 1980. A lot of damage happened when rubble cascaded from the top, damaging the homes beneath.

Rural rumblings

Earthquakes obviously cause a lot of deaths in cities, where there are high concentrations of people. In more rural areas, whole towns and villages can be totally wiped out. The people living in them are usually farming communities. It would be far too difficult for them to uproot themselves and find more land in a safer place. In the southern Mediterranean region especially, getting out of harm's way is not an option, as so much of the area lies in a danger zone. In 1908, the Sicilian town of Messina and the surrounding countryside was struck by an earthquake that reached about 7.5 on the **Richter scale**. Small towns and villages were totally flattened – 58 000 people died. On top of this tragedy the agricultural economy was wrecked, with few people left to revitalize it.

Where next?

It isn't always obvious where the next big earthquake will strike. On the map on page 4 we can see a large area to the east of the Rocky Mountains in the United States, known as the Midwest. It does not lie on the San Andreas fault line but there are over 100 other lines, and folds disguising the **reverse faults** that lie beneath them. There has not been a serious earthquake in this region since 1812, but there have been several thousand tremors. **Seismologists** believe that a widespread quake of at least **magnitude** 7 on the Richter scale is likely to strike within the next 50 years. The American Midwest is farming country. There are also several major cities in the region. If a large earthquake did strike, it would be disastrous for both humans and agriculture. However, the earth could just as easily rumble away for a hundred years or more without any major problem.

Rescue under the rubble

Shattered services

Many victims of earthquake disasters are rescued by search teams from other countries, using trained sniffer dogs and heat-sensitive equipment to locate people buried under the rubble. This is because local transport, **communications** and emergency services have been severely damaged.

Burst water pipes prevent water from being pumped up to put out fires. Fractured gas pipes and ruptured electricity cables can cause widespread fires. These can explode into fire storms – flames roar upwards sucking in air underneath, fanning them in 160 kilometre per hour (100 miles per hour) blow-torch winds. Other problems facing rescue teams and aid agencies are aftershocks, disease brought about by contaminated water supplies and lack of shelter.

Earthquake education

Panic kills. Japan has recognized that its people need to know what to do in an earthquake, so that orderly **evacuation** can take place. In earthquake training centres, people are taught what to do if an earthquake strikes. Some are placed in a room set on a moving floor. The floor shakes to simulate tremors, furniture slides about, crockery crashes to the floor. People are trained to turn off the gas flame on the cooker, switch off electrical appliances, place special hats on their heads and masks over mouths and noses, and then to crawl under the table. In addition towns, villages and cities all over Japan hold an earthquake preparation day each year, which includes first aid courses.

Pressure points

The problems below that faced Armenia after the December 1988 earthquake show just how difficult it is for poorer nations to cope. In all 700 000 people were affected by the earthquake, 100 000 of whom died.

- Many of the buildings in Armenia were poorly constructed from concrete that tends to crumble – many more buildings fell than would normally be expected from an earthquake measuring 6.9 on the **Richter scale**.

- Rescue attempts were made difficult by poor transport and communications.

- International search teams, with special tracing equipment and dogs, arrived only after the first two days. Until this time, only untrained rescuers tried to find survivors.

- Hospitals had been damaged and medical staff killed.

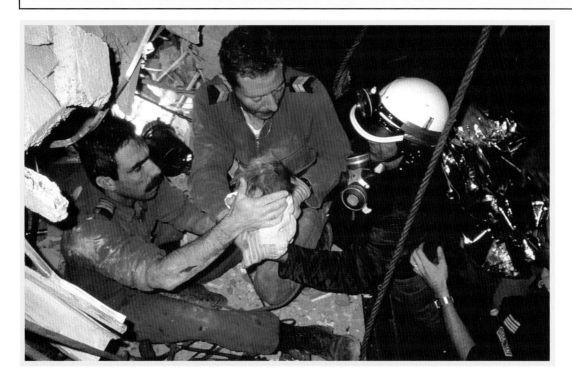

Miracles do happen. This is all that is left of a hospital that collapsed during the Mexico City earthquake disaster of 1985. But among the rubble, a whole week after the catastrophe, new-born babies were being pulled out alive.

37

Design for survival

One of the most important ways in which we can improve the chances of survival in a powerful earthquake is to make sure our buildings stay upright.

Better buildings

Architects, engineers and builders have been building with earthquakes in mind for several centuries. After the 1509 earthquake in Turkey, the government invested a lot of money to ensure that mosques were all built with reinforced arches and strengthened curved ceilings and domes.

However, even today, in many parts of the Mediterranean and the Middle East, houses are often built of thick, heavy stone or earthen walls, with roofs supported by large beams. The thick walls might seem very protective, but they are not strengthened by supports and can still collapse in a deadly heap. However, traditional houses in villages in southern Portugal have two interesting features. One is an inward slant to the outside part of the extremely thick walls, which props up the inner section. The other feature is the roof, which is lined with lightweight bamboo canes and poles which would not be too destructive if they fell.

This elegant building in Lisbon's Praca do Comercio was built immediately after the devastating earthquake of 1755. It was built with fire-resistant partitions and reinforced walls.

Modern methods

Nowadays, architects and engineers in earthquake zones make shock-resistance a priority. Some tall buildings are set on floating bases which absorb the energy of a tremor. Electronically-controlled **counterweights** are attached to the top. These rock away from the direction of the shake, stopping the building from swaying. Other buildings are set on rubber or steel pads, raising them from ground. This helps them to cope when the ground is pulled sideways. Special building materials – metals and concrete – are created to absorb shocks. New types of shatter-resistant glass are being developed.

Inside, large buildings also have to be designed so that there are enough clear exits and fire-escapes. In Los Angeles, equipment has been developed for making sure that furniture and fittings stay in place when the room shakes.

One of the most important considerations is the land on which buildings are constructed. This must not be too soft and loose, or it will lead to **liquefaction** (see page 7). Nor must it lie on top of hidden cracks.

There was massive damage to the Kiteko Dam Complex in Kobe, Japan during the earthquake in 1995.

Shaking nature

Harming homes and habitats

When the Earth shakes and splits it takes the lives of plants and animals and alters the face of their natural habitats. Birds' nests, wasps' nests, beehives, rabbit warrens, badger dens, beaver lodges – all these are destroyed when an earthquake cracks open the land. Adults and young can be buried, or the mating and nest-building season may be disturbed. Animals can be forced out of **hibernation** in cold weather, before food is available for them to eat. Creatures that **estivate** – or sleep during very hot weather – are forced to the surface where the temperatures are too extreme for them to survive.

During an earthquake, the land surface can be broken up or covered by landslides. Severe and prolonged shaking uproots trees and bushes. The US state of Mississippi shook for over a year between 1811 and 1812 – three tremors reached over 8 on the **Richter scale**. Many trees toppled over as their roots loosened in the soil. Massive land **subsidence** and uplift ripped apart rivers and streams, leaving aquatic plants and animals high and dry. The Mississippi quakes were so disturbing that a river temporarily flowed the wrong way!

These delicate sea creatures need seawater to wash over them regularly. In 1822 a huge earthquake along coastal Chile thrust a section of the seashore upwards by over a metre (3.3 feet) exposing beds of oysters, mussels, and seaweeds. They all dried out in the baking sun.

Tall stories?

We know that animals seem to sense earthquakes. There are many more strange tales to tell – of catfish that dance around wildly, of rats that rush up to attics a week before an earth tremor and of stray cats that just disappear off the streets. An hour before the 1989 San Francisco earthquake, pigeons were too nervous to leave their coops.

These stories might seem doubtful, but researchers have found that it is definitely possible for creatures to sense quakes. It has been discovered that bees are deeply disturbed by the moving forces under the ground. This may be because the **magnetite** in their bodies, which in normal circumstances helps them to find their location, reacts strongly to **electromagnetic** waves. Honeybees are especially sensitive. All animals have certain levels of magnetite – and so do we!

A **tsunami** can can cover a beach with sand, mud and other debris, as well as completely destroying animal life and natural habitats. This is a beach at Miami in Florida after a tsunami.

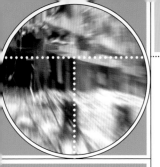

Earthquakes in history

Where's the evidence?

All over the world there is evidence of ancient earthquakes – huge land-slips, cracks and thrusts scar the landscape, while folded mountains bear witness to the churning Earth.

Radio-carbon dating can reveal if and when remains of ancient vegetation on a lower piece of land once grew on a level with rock that now towers above. Scientists look for traces of a type of carbon, called 'carbon-14' in decayed or fossilized plants that they find in both the lower and upper parts of slipped land. The carbon breaks down at a known rate, so by measuring the amount of carbon-14 still in the plant matter, scientists can find out how long ago the plants were alive. Sometimes scientists may also find the same animal and plant fossils on different land levels, which shows that at one time the surface was flat.

Seismologists in history

It has taken a long time for scientists to work out how earthquakes happen and they still do not know everything. The **plate tectonic** theory was completed only 30 years ago, but the mystery of earthquakes has puzzled scientists since ancient times. The Greek philosopher and scientist, Aristotle, believed that earthquakes were caused by trapped air exploding from beneath the ground. Modern theories only emerged after the development of instruments that could measure sound waves under the Earth's surface. One of the first was made in 1883 by an English mechanical engineer and geologist, John Milne. It was a **seismograph** powered by clockwork.

Pressure points

- Deposits in the US state of Washington's mudflats reveal that the area was once swamped by a massive **tsunami** wave.

- A 20-centimetre (8-inch) sand deposit was dumped by a tsunami several kilometres inland from the Scottish coast of Montrose 7000 years ago. The deposits were discovered in 1974 by students from Coventry University in England.

- Chunks of land snapped off the Hawaiian Islands, probably over 100 000 years ago. This probably caused tsunami waves 300 metres (about 980 feet) high as far as Australia, Japan or the United States.

Over the next 70 years, using a network of seismic instruments, an accurate world map of faultlines was drawn. It was remarkably similar to one constructed by an Irish civil engineer, Robert Mallet, in 1857, without using any instruments. He had mapped all the earthquake evidence available to him through geological studies and eyewitness accounts. Although his map is incomplete, it is very much like modern faultline maps. His studies helped modern scientists to work out that most earth tremors occur along **tectonic plates**.

These are the earthquake-shattered ruins of the Temple of Apollo in Corinth, Greece. All around the Mediterranean and Middle East, crumbled ancient cities are evidence of devastating earthquake activity.

Earth-shattering earthquakes

Top ten most deadly earthquakes

Earthquakes have many different effects. It is impossible even to guess at the strength of early earthquakes, and difficult to count how many people have been killed by them. No list can be truly accurate.

Location of earthquake	Date	Number of people killed
Shanshi, China	23 Jan 1556	830 000
Calcutta, India	11 Oct 1737	300 000
Tangshan, China	27 July 1976	242 000
Aleppo, Syria	9 August 1138	230 000
Damghan, Iran	22 December 856	200 000
Gansu, China	16 December 1920	200 000
Nan-Shan, China	22 May 1927	200 000
Ardabil, Iran	23 March 893	150 000
Kanto Plain, Japan	1 September 1923	142 807
Chihli, China	September 1290	100 000

Pressure points

- Two million people were killed by earthquakes in the 20th century alone – but in total, there was only one hour of major earthquake shaking.

- There could be millions of earthquakes every year worldwide but only a small number (about 120) of them will cause destruction. Hundreds will cause minor damage.

- The largest earthquake recorded reached 9.5 on the **moment magnitude** scale in Chile on 2 May 1960. Many cities were badly damaged, the **shock wave** was 10 metres (33 feet) high and an area of land 850 kilometres (530 miles) long and 130 kilometres (80 miles) wide cracked open.

In October 1997 a series of shocks hit the town of Assisi in Italy. The 700-year-old basilica was slightly damaged. It contains precious wall paintings – or frescoes – created by a famous artist called Giotto. While people were examining the damage a huge aftershock struck the basilica. Four people died, and the frescoes were shattered. The photo on page 44 shows the moment of collapse. The tiny pieces were gathered together and – astoundingly – the works have been restored.

Glossary

accelerometer   measures huge tremors that are too big for seismometers – and possibly would destroy the seismometer

body wave   a group of energy waves that move through solid, even rock

breakwater   a concrete barrier built near the coast to break up large, destructive waves before they can cause damage on the shore

channel   the course carved into rock by a river or stream

compression   the first half of an energy wave – it pulses outwards like a ripple in a pond (see also 'elastic rebound')

communications   facilities like roads, railways and telephone lines

conduit   a channel that leads from a volcano's magma chamber to the vent

counterweight   a weight used to balance out the weight of an object

elastic rebound   the second half of an energy wave – it causes stress on rock, deforming it. When the strain is too great the force is released in a sudden jerk – and the rock is reshaped (see also 'compression').

electromagnetic, electromagnetism a magnetic force which is caused by an electric current

epicentre   the point on the Earth's surface that lies directly on top of the fault movement deep down in the Earth's crust. Shock waves travel outwards from the epicentre.

estivate   when a creature sleeps and its body slows down during very hot months of the year

evacuate   to move people to safety

fault creep   tiny movements of sections of the Earth's crust

fissures   cracks in the Earth's crust

focus   (more than one = foci) where the original fault movement occurs

frequency   the number of waves passing point within a certain time

geologist   a scientist who studies rocks, minerals and rock formations

geyser   a jet of hot water, which spurts up from hot volcanic rock beneath the surface of the Earth

Global Telemetred Seismograph Network   computerized satellite-linked worldwide earthquake monitoring system

granite   a hard rock with a uniform texture

hazard map   a map showing the areas most likely to experience earthquake disaster, and therefore the most dangerous to live in

hibernate, hibernation   when a creature sleeps and its body slows down during very cold months of the year

hot spring   a spring heated by hot, volcanic rock beneath the Earth's surface

infrasound   minute wavelengths of sound that humans cannot hear

infrastructure   means of communications, transport and services, such as roads, railways, electricity, drains

insurance policy   a promise by an insurance company to pay for damage caused to property by a disaster – the owner of the property has to make regular payments to the insurance company

intensity   the number on a scale measuring the amount of energy being released by a seismic wave

interfere   when two or more waves meet they may combine to strengthen each other, or cancel each other out

lava   hot, molten rock that oozes or flows above the Earth's surface

liquefaction   when a tremor shakes soft or loose rock so much that it moves around like a liquid

magma chamber   a well of magma that seeps up into the Earth's crust

magma   the hot, sticky molten rock that makes up the mantle – it oozes or flows beneath the Earth's crust

magnetite   magnetic iron ore

magnitude   the amount of energy released by seismic waves that radiate from the epicentre of an earthquake

mantle   the hot, sticky layer of molten rock which surrounds the Earth and on which the Earth's crust sits

moment magnitude   an earthquake measurement that considers the type of rock in which the fault moves, the amount of land over which the fault has moved and the average length of the fault movement

offset   a dramatic sideways movement on the Earth's surface

Pacific Tsunami Warning System (PTWS)   an earthquake monitoring system that predicts tsunami waves anywhere within the Pacific Basin – the system is located in Hawaii

plate tectonics   the study of the tectonic plates (see below) that make up the Earth's crust

pressure wave   a body wave (see above) that moves lengthways through material along the crust

radio-carbon dating   measuring the deterioration of a special carbon (carbon 14) in decayed plant matter to work out how old the plant matter is

reverse fault   a backward-sloping fault – often hidden by folds of rock above

Richter scale   a scale that gives values for the amount of energy released by seismic waves radiating from the epicentre – invented by US seismologist, Dr Charles Richter, in 1935

sediment   soft rock or soil particles deposited by water

seismic motion   the length and size of a tremor

seismic wave   a wave of energy that makes the material through which it moves tremble

seismograph   an instrument that traces the pattern of ground tremors onto a paper roll or a magnetic tape – the pattern is registered by a seismometer

seismologist   a scientist who studies movements in the Earth's crust

seismology   the study of movements in the Earth's crust

seismometer   an instrument that picks up the pattern of ground tremors

shear wave   a body wave that moves across the direction of the final quake

shock wave   a wave of energy rippling outward from the epicentre

subduction zone   the place where one edge of the Earth's crust slips down beneath the opposite edge

submerged   covered with something – such as water or rubble

subsidence   when a section of the Earth sinks

surface wave   a group of energy waves that move along irregular parts of rock structures – bands and layers of different types of rock

tectonic plate   a huge slab of the Earth's crust that sits on the mantle; the plates move apart and together, sometimes rubbing against each other; plates are separated by deep trenches

tide gauge   an instrument that measures changes in the height of ocean tides and sea level

tsunami   a series of high ocean waves caused by earthquakes, volcanic activity or landslides vibrating against seawater

vent   the opening inside the volcano through which the magma errupts

vulcanologist   a scientist who studies volcanic activity

Index